OVERCOME DEPRESSION IN ONE HOUR

BY: TONY SMITH

Introduction- Life is Happening, Why Rejoice?

Stop It! Just Stop It, she exclaimed as the slim shadow of my dark smoky presence filled the aura of her personal space. At that moment, I froze like a deer tranced by the dancing of the headlights across the horizon. Instantly, I knew this was going to be no ordinary encounter. I drew closer armed with an effervescent smile and a precocious spirit aimed at understanding the environment around me. She recoiled like a rattlesnake taunting her victim ever so slightly in the misty distance. I was returning to college for my sophomore year at Oakwood College after spending a glorious Christmas break in the sunny state of Florida. The preferred transport of choice for a broke and fabulous college student was Greyhound Bus Lines- where the slogan is 'leave the driving to us'. Well in theory that sounded good but I was faced with a 20 hour trip back to campus on this particular occasion. Every moment of it sure to be filled with babies crying, the smatter of small talk and rain pelting the window taunting the morning sunshine as it dries off the tears from heaven.

I had made it to my presumed halfway point, a Montgomery, AL rest stop, and it was here with my earphones plodded on and causally browsing around in the bus terminal that I was confronted by this woman. I finally mustered up the courage to say 'Hi, your name is? Forgive me, but what is it that you want me to stop doing?' She retracted a bit, skipped over my first question, and coyly answered 'Why are you so h appy?' The synapses of my mind were racing around and around like the circular loading button on a Windows laptop searching for an answer to this question. Finally after a momentous pause, I replied 'I am not happy just joyful and reminiscing about the times spent with my family and friends over the holidays. She paused for a moment as and said 'So how come you be joyful, don't you realize that life is happening all around us?' 'These past few months have been unbearable for me, I have lost my job at a plant making tires and my eighteen year old son is moving out and joining the Navy this year. Things for me cannot get any worse'. 'I cannot begin to understand how you feel', I replied

2

emphatically. But this I do know, replying confidently, 'we can rejoice in knowing that God holds our future in the palms of his hands'. She placed a stick of gum in her mouth and replied 'Life is happening to me, why should I rejoice?' The crisp winter air kissed my lips shut as she walked away toward another bus awaiting her transfer to Texas her final destination for the evening. At that moment, I realized that everlasting joy in this life is a precious and hard sought after commodity. I was blessed to be able to taste the blessings of joy on more than one occasion thus far in my life but still I longed for a deeper experience with God and the joy that I knew only he can give to me.

Is Happiness overrated? If happiness was a drug that I could take every day, would I want to take it? I submit to you today that happiness is indeed overrated. Happiness can be defined as the temporary feeling or experience of pleasure or elation. In this world, many young people have proclaimed their intentions of 'I just want to be happy, no matter what!'. It is this YOLO (You only live once) declaration to the world that if I must go through with the ups and downs of life at least I can make myself happy.

I declare to you today that the best medicine for depression is everlasting joy. Happiness is dependent upon circumstances with are ever changing and never ending. It is the temporary at best and it allows for one to continue going from happiness "high" to another without fully embracing the event which led to your temporary feeling of euphoria.

Furthermore, happiness is simply more of a manufactured emotion and it is event based. Joy is based on a Person and/or an experience with a Person (Jesus Christ) and that it turn is helps us to have joyous experiences with each other as well. The best remedy for feeling out of sync in this world is getting in touch with the One who is acquainted with all of your feelings, emotions, and plans for the future. Jesus says in John 15:11 NKJV "These things I have spoken unto you that My joy may remain in you and that your joy may be full."

Now I must confess to you that I am a "rookie" joy addict. There were times in my life where I swallowed the pill of happiness by faking to like people who I did not like, buying more toys like video games and more computer hardware, and other useless things to appease the fumes rising up from my empty soul. I also must confess that on this journey to joy, there will be some pain and some moments where joy seems as elusive as catching a bubble before it pops in your face. But I promise you that this journey will be worth it, because as it has been said 'Anyone worth having is difficult'.

So with that in mind, I invite you to join me on this journey to everlasting joy and let's become addicted to everlasting joy forever in Christ. So in the words of my friend who asked that night in the bus terminal 'Life is happening, why Rejoice?'. Throughout our journey together, we will use the acronym REJOICE to highlight 7 principles from Gods word and the experiences of His prophets to help shed insight into the everlasting joy that led them through the dark corridors of depression, fear, and self-doubt. The REJOICE acronym stands for these seven principles: **R**ecognize, **E**xpect, **J**ust Pray, **O**pen your Heart, **I**nvest in Yourself and Others, **C**ut out Negative Thoughts and People, and **E**xhale all stress away and enjoy your life.

Chapter 1 I'm Sick and Tired of Being Sick and Tired

Bam, Clunk, Clunk, Clunk, Pop, Boom… these were the sounds of my car as it slowly died in the middle of an eight lane interstate highway. I was stranded!! I was alone, tired, and possibly preparing to say goodbye to Nina (my car) for the last time. It had been one of those days- the kind where mismatched dress socks, burnt toast, clogged highways, and grumpy people standing in line for mocha express matching their darkness of their mood in the morning.

A rainy Friday afternoon where the clouds draped its way over my heart like a blanket bathed in Velcro. It had not been just a bad day but a bad week and month for that matter. I had learned that the job that I had applied for had been axed due to budgetary cutbacks. My girlfriend at the time offered no such support at the time and any reconciliation on the horizon looked about as sure as an Ike and Tina reunion concert.

I slowly popped the hood only to find a tangled mass of fluids and a web of smoke filling the interior cabin. This can't be happening to me, I had planned on using my tax return for something more constructive than fixing my car. Why does it seem like the mishaps always occur around a time of blessing? At last, a dusty blue truck pulled up behind my stalled car. I cringed for a second thinking *not only is my car going to be out of commission, I might be too!* Luckily, I recognized the Miami Dolphin front license plate and knew it was one of my friends from church. I breathed a sigh of relief and headed out of my car to greet the tall lanky fellow. 'Seems like you are stuck huh?' Yeah I said and it does not look good for Nina. 'Do you have

AAA towing' he inquired 'No' I said affirmatively 'Well good luck trying to get it fixed, I have to go pick up my daughter from school, I'll be praying for you brother' Are you serious? I don't need your prayers right now, I need a ride home which would only require twenty minutes of your time!!

I stood there like a puppy dog waiting for his owner to return after taking his toy away for being bad. I was upset and frustrated. I called my sister to come pick me up after she got off from work. After two hours of waiting, I was finally home. I had lost everything I worked for thus far, my car was found to have broken timing belt damaging the pistons, my girlfriend broke up with me, and my so called friends have morphed like child-like acquaintances.

It is one thing to come to be doing all of the wrong things and still be blessed, but what if you are doing everything right and still not happy? Where is the joy then? Is this the plan of God for my life at this moment?

One of my favorite passages in the Bible is the story of David and his men when they approached the camp at Ziglag. It is found in 1 Samuel 30 in your Bible. David had lost everything during the battle with the Amalekites. Imagine having your wife and kids taken captive, not killed, not tortured, and without a proverbial ransom note leaving outlandish demands. David found himself not knowing whether he was coming or going in this predicament.

David was greatly distressed and helplessly depressed as anyone would be facing both the hallowing cries of agony billowing from his own heart and the wails of his men breathing the thin air of solace to no avail. All of his men around him were equally depressed and they spoke of killing David. David and his men wept until they had no more power to weep.

Lessons learned from this encounter

One of the first principles on this journey to joy and wholeness is to recognize that you are not alone in experiencing moments of depression, doubt, and anxiety in this world. When we recognize that we are depressed and are tired of being in that state, then we are ready to do something positive about our situation. David and his men wept together until all of the emotions built up inside had been totally released. David and his men had been sick and tired of being sick and tired. You know there is much freedom in releasing oneself from one's own feelings of entrapment, defeat, and discouragement. The next verse states that "David then encouraged Himself in the Lord"

Sometimes when all of our support systems are gone, it is okay to recognize that we are depressed and vent out our frustrations in healthy ways. It is okay to get angry sometimes. Too many people feel that angry feelings is a dirty stain that should only be shown when something bad is done to them.

When I was playing baseball, my dad always told me to keep my head up towards the sky when attempting to catch the ball. I did not listen and would constantly be looking down at the ground the ball would hit me in the head instead of in my glove. Sometimes in life we have to adjust our vision to look up at God for He is always waiting to do a new thing in our lives if we place ourselves in the right position.

When you are tired of looking down, you will look up. Look up to the hills from which comes your help, your Help is from the Lord. I had to recognize that I was not alone in my struggle in battling negative thoughts and people. I also recognized like David that the best help came from God who is always seeking for me to be a part of His team of glory. There was nothing that I could do wrong to be cast away from His sight or plans for my life in spite of the present circumstances.

After David's praise session with the Lord, he then sought to avenge the losses that the Amalekites had inflicted upon he and his men by redeeming the time lost at hand. David recovered everything, including wives and children, that day and the people were grateful. The Lord is waiting to restore you today but allow a place for him in your life today. Will you recognize your need for Christ so that he can restore you to everlasting joy today? Join me on this journey to healing and restoration as we continue to REJOICE (Recognize, Expect, Just Pray, Open Your Heart, Invest Time, Cut out Negativity, and Exhale Stress) always in any circumstance.

JoyRX Questions to Consider

1. What feelings are you avoiding or harboring without expressing them to someone?

2. What is the one change that you can make today that will help you feel better in the long run?

3. When was the last time you recognized someone else and encouraged them through their journey?

Chapter 2- Are You Expecting or Explaining?

Have you ever tried to explain yourself to others and wasted more energy than you wanted? Why do actions or getting results speak louder than words? When I was younger, fishing was a favorite pastime to do with my dad and brother. There we were paddling through a glistening farm pond with the smell of fish teasing our noses as we waited for fish to come to our location. Fishing did not start out as a love affair for me. Fishing for us was usually conducted in the rain. Yes, rain!! Apparently, my dad thinks that we are ducks looking for worms rather than fish! But seriously, it has been noted to be one of the best times to catch fish during an early morning or evening rain shower. Try explaining that to a 13 year old video game crazed kid. A small tin metal boat and paddling everywhere for hours trolling for fish that acted like secret agents with a cloak of invisible smile to match. It was muggy, three hours passed, and mosquitoes were putting in their orders like a drive thru on my skinny dusty arms. 'Dad, where are the fish? I moaned as I wiped drops of rain from my lenses. 'Be patient, Anthony, I know fish are in this area because I have been here before'. Yeah right, he must have ate too many granola energy bars because the only thing that going to be jumping in this water is me heading back to shore, I said to myself. I could hear the echoes of chatter and nonchalant fritter by other family members 'I don't know why they are wasting their time in the rain, maybe they are trying to take an early bath!' Another uncle jovially taunts 'I think the last time he caught anything worthwhile was your mom!' Oh the joys of family! We were expected to catch the most fish as we can for the fish fry that was upcoming.

The steady rain began to ease to a misty drizzle and our moods began to lift as little as well. Well my mood raised because I figured we only would have two hours of daylight left to fish. 'Hey there is a spot that my friend fished yesterday back behind two fallen trees that had fish' my brother shouted. Well my dad agreed to go and so we paddled for ten minutes to the spot. Algae covered the top of the water like a welcome mat begging us to tread through it for something valuable. We baited our poles and switched our bait to ones that would float on top of the water.

'I got one!!' I got one', said my brother 'Got what?' I said hoping that he did not get his line stuck for the one hundredth time! 'A fish' My heart was beating faster than a locomotive pulling into port and I grabbed the net to scoop up with I hoped was a fish. It was not just any fish but a 5 pound largemouth bass! That day we caught four more bass in that same area. I joked about fish and now here at 7pm, a full eight hours later, we have something to show for our efforts- fish! All of the wasted bait, stuck lines in trees, mosquito bites, paddling, dry granola bars, and rain showers could not wipe away the smile from my face as we approached shore. I learned that day that sometimes it is best to follow your instinct or "gut feeling" even if the expected outcome smells "fishy" to others. God specializes into making the unconventional, conventional.

Sometimes people, instead of moving forward with their God inspired plans, worry about what others are going to think about what they are doing. This paralyzes them like a deer in headlights to do anything constructive with what God has given them to use for the benefit of others. If my dad would have listened to others and not fished in the rain, then the fish fry would not have been a reality for our family. The fish are not magically jumping up on our plates for they are happy living their lives swimmingly I guarantee you! There is however another person in the Bible that was not praying for fish but for a son.

In 1 Samuel 1, there is a lady named Hannah who was one of the wives of Elkanah. She prayed to God night and day because she did not have any children. The Lord closed up her womb. I can imagine Elkanah's other wife walking by day after day flaunting her kids in the face of Hannah like a parade of pride down Main Street. Hannah being taunted incessantly even by her own husband who just could not understand why she would be crying night and day. Hannah was so focused on receiving her blessing from the Lord that she did not even want to eat! Hannah goes to the local marketplace and the chatter of the woman around her 'Why is she buying papyrus diapers for a baby she does not have yet?' 'Why is she praying to God for? Does she not know it is too late for her to have kids' Hannah was expecting to receive a blessing from the Lord and she knew that explaining to others would take all the energy she needed to stay focused on the mission. How many of us take our eyes of our mission from God in order to answer the expectations of others? Don't let the expectations of others for your life cause you to miss out on the blessings that God has planned for your life.

So the first thing that struck me about Hannah was that she was a seeker who constantly expected that God would come through for her in the clutch-the eleventh hour. It was not a naïve prayer of faith but one grounded in what God has done for her in the past.

What are you so focused on today that would cause you not to eat? In this society, child bearing was a sign of honor and dignity for a woman. Hannah's friends and cohorts probably thought she crazy for spending so much time praying for a son when her womb was closed. But she remained focused on running her race with God. Sometimes God calls us to be that "lone ranger" challenging Him on His promises that He has never failed to meet at any time on this terrestrial ball called Earth.

Furthermore, God wants us to expect the best blessings for us like Hannah we must be ready to move forward with our plans so that God may bless our efforts. You cannot afford to allow the opinions, expectations, or even visions of others to paralyze your mission that God has uniquely given to you to fulfill. I love to play basketball pickup games at the local park. It is not the NBA but everyone is playing to win and expects you to contribute something toward that goal. One day, I was wide open for a three pointer but passed the ball back to the middle point guard because I was afraid of missing that shot. Later, the point guard pulled me aside and told me the famous quote by Wayne Gretzy "You miss 100 percent of the shots you don't take". It is imperative that we take action with confidence on the vision God has shown us whether through His word or through others. Don't waste too much of your energy about explaining to others your gifts, talents, and vision from God.

Finally, Hannah dedicated herself to preparing to receive the blessing from the Lord. Hannah was not afraid to be vulnerable before God and man. As a result, God honored her request with Samuel being born shortly thereafter. It takes the prayer of faith to move mountains that man say have no place being moved in the first place. God is willing to do it for us, but we have to ask Him in prayer to help us to remove all doubt, whether self-doubt or doubt placed on your shoulders by others, in order to have a successful outcome. Will you pray with me that God will teach us to expect more from Him and take Him at His word today?

JoyRX Action Questions

1. What would you do in life if you were not worried about what some people would say or do?

2. Do you expect God to bless you even in the little things like gas money or food for your children on a weekly basis?

3. When was the last time you motivated someone else to live their dreams in Christ?

Chapter 3- Just Bend Those Knees!

Do you ever feel like your prayers are bouncing off the ceiling faster than a ping pong ball? Do you often find yourself talking about what you are going to do and not actually doing it?

I remember when I graduated from college and I got my first job in Florida. The warm air would kiss my cheeks as I walked toward the train waiting to take me home every sunset. I loved my job, at least I put on a front that I did, but the problem was not my job. I did not have a car to get to work and it was so painstaking waiting for my friend to pick me up and drop me off was not my idea of independent living. Who would have thought that at the ripe old age of 22, I would just be getting my first car when some kids have that at 18 years of age.

I searched day and night looking for the perfect new used car. Yes a used car is new to me. I had finally found it- a great looking Honda that I spotted at a little independent used dealership. It had everything I wanted and more and looked clean on both the inside and outside. It would not only serve my needs but also I could pick up my little sister from school as well. There was only one problem lurking in the room- money!! I did not have money for the down payment or been on my job long enough to have a credit history. That Friday night I went home and printed out a color copy of that car in high definition and stuck it on my bedroom wall. I photo shopped a picture of myself in the driver seat window as extra motivation. I prayed to God to give me that car and to let it be a blessing not just to me and my family but to others who I would likely come into contact in that town. I also prayed that the small dealership would not try to rip me off but work with me in a fair and no hassle manner. You know you have to pray for those you meet before even they meet you, you never know how the Holy Spirit might move. I rose off my knees that night and it was if God spoke to me and said 'How bad do you want it, Anthony? It won't be easy but if you work hard, it is yours to have'. I began to sketch a financial plan or budget or Sunday using my computer software program and I gave myself about six to eight weeks to save money for the down payment.

Three weeks had past and I only had about a third of the money needed. I went to prayer meeting and all of my friends inquired 'So you're going to buy a car and you have what 350 dollars?' You need a lot more than that, they scoffed. I was a little discouraged because this was not the idle chatter of acquaintances tickling my ears but words cutting through the air faster than a hummingbird's wings from my inner circle of friends. I had expected a prayer or the proverbial 'I will pray for you my brother' greeting after all it was after "prayer meeting".

Despite the air of negativity and pensive doubt around me, I continued to pursue my dream car with groom like eyes fixed on his beaming bride in the distance. I only had eyes for that Honda. I brought items for it in advance like tire shine, wax, steering wheel cover, and other accessories that would make it look outstanding. I proudly flaunted pictures of it to my brother, sister, mother, father, and anyone who would enter my room. God's affirmation that many nights ago was all that I needed to press forward. Sometimes all it takes is one Person to be in your corner for everything to be alright in any circumstance.

As the weeks eroded away, I felt as if my money goals were slowly inching along like a snail with no legs. But suddenly, I received a call from my dad in which he informed me that the credit union, of which he was a member, might be willing to give me a loan for the car. I snuffed at the idea at first because I did not think that would consider my request but I asked for the loan application materials to be sent to me anyway. One week passed and they approved my request

15

and now I just had to test drive the car and make sure everything was up to par. God has a thousand ways to bless us and He sometimes uses the people we least expect to bless or encourage us to continue on in the journey.

One such man in the Bible that overcome dire circumstances by prayer and faith is a man named Jabez. His life story is short and is noted in 1 Chronicles 4:9-10. Jabez whose very name given by his mother means "he will cause pain" or "sorrowful" in Hebrew was given from the start a t birth by his mother. Imagine people walking down the street calling out 'Here comes that pain maker!' Even still, hearing the taunts and jests of his brothers predicting him to be a failure and the bane of the all their problems. Names held significant meaning in ancient times on one's destiny or life.

But thank God that there is one Name that Jabez knew he could call on to help him from the beginning. He knew that prayer is the only wireless connection that is free, has no downtime, and the signal is always strong no matter how far distanced he felt from God at that time. Jabez prayed a prayer of faith and hope that would sustain him throughout his whole life.

When examining this story, there are three main lessons that helped me in my prayer journey. First, Jabez looked to God first to change his situation for the better. He did not draw up strategic plans to change his own destiny or take matters into his own hands. He was not satisfied with living a mediocre life as the text notes "he was more honorable than his brothers" in v.9. The other brothers and the sons of Judah are listed but only Jabez is recorded as reaching out to God for more in spite of present circumstances.

Furthermore, it is sometimes through our pain and suffering that we are able to express our deepest and authentic prayers to God. God sometimes does his best work in painful and hopeless situations. Jabez knew that he did not have time to beat around the bush, his fate was known to all around him as being the "one who causes pain". But the only heart he is concerned about causing pain was God's heart.

Finally, Jabez prayed not only that God would keep himself from evil and pain but that his territory would be enlarged. Jabez prayed for others, including his brothers and his mother, that he would be a blessing to them all the days of his life. Sometimes prayer is more about changing the lives and perspectives of others than it is about changing our own lives. Jabez was committed to speaking blessing to others via prayer and was not afraid to ask for this in prayer up front.

What plans and dreams are you not telling God about today? What would it take for you to just pray first about all areas of your life? Like Jabez, we too can reach those who might have written us off by showing love and praying for their blessing as well as our own at the same time. Just pray, God is always waiting to perform a miracle in your life today! Can you see the possibilities?

JoyRX Action Questions

1. When was the last time you prayed for something that was not an urgent or dire request of your heart?

2. Is prayer an option among many for you or the only option for success and peace of mind?

3. How often during the weeks/months have you prayed for those you don't know in your community who you suspect might be facing challenges alone?

Chapter 4 Can you see the Possibilities?

Ugh! It's raining again! This should not be happening on a relaxed Wednesday afternoon in Florida. You see the weather and I have a love-hate relationship. It is something that I hated dealing with during my high school days. I can remember planning dates for a young lady to an outdoor jazz summer concert only to be rained out by a storm coming. Or even trying to attend a game only to be canceled by a tropical storm that flirted with us like a bull fighter holding that red thing around and around in the sky. Imagine that-hurricanes in Florida!! Ahh, who would dream of something so universal being such a heartbreaker to my plans for fun and relaxation.

The weather was a nuisance to me because I knew that it was one of the areas that affected my daily life that I had no control over whatsoever. It was unpredictable and it required me to adjust on the fly like a cheap umbrella being bashed by the invisible gusts of wind exposing its wiry frame for all to see in the streets. To make matters even worse, the meteorologist paints a hopeless picture of rain by adding rain percentages to the forecast. For example, there is a 90 percent chance that you are going to see rain in your area by the end of the day. This means that rain is almost guaranteed to arrive at your back porch at any time during the day. I spent many days moaning and groaning about the weather and like clockwork I would guess when the typical Florida afternoon showers would rumble in off the Atlantic Ocean.

But after a while, I began to pour my heart into discovering the reasons behind why weather behaves the way that it does. I checked out a stack of weather related library books from the local library and read up on all the different weather I was experiencing in my area and how I would have to adjust to it appropriately. It felt relieving to open my heart to the possibility that the weather was not out to make my life miserable.

I discovered that the rain does not always fall in the same location twice. When the weather forecaster states that there is a 50 percent chance of rain, he or she means that in our coverage area, there is a 50 percent chance of rain. This means that it is very possible that 50 percent will see rain and 50 percent will not see rain. This was great news to me because now on the weekends I could have one morning to stay in and one evening to go out with friends. The sun is still present even when it is raining, it's just higher than what we can see at the moment due to clouds and obvious visibility. How many opportunities for blessings have you missed due to the apparent rains of life blocking your view of the Sun? Could the Son still help you in the midst of rain? If we open our hearts fully to God like an umbrella waving to the sky, He will bring us toward unexpected blessings, results, or plans for our lives.

I was ecstatic to discover that Jesus cares even about the most minuscule parts of my day to help me adjust to the rain showers in my daily life. I now love the weather because I see the possibilities in the rain, in the sunshine, the lights of wisdom glistening through the fog, and invisible wind cooling me down as a walk down a dusty street. I love the feeling that rushes through my body that Jesus can take the fog of anxiety and worry and clear it away into peace and calmness of mind.

In life, we sometimes skip over the trees to get to the open meadows. In other words, we do not consider using what is already in front of us to accomplish our dreams in life. It can be uncomfortable to think outside of the box and stand out from the crowd. But this is precisely where the gold at the end of the rainbow lies.

God has given each one of us a unique and gifted skillset to use for His glory. This toolbox does not come prepackaged the same for everyone on this terrestrial ball called Earth. For starters, many people's talents would grow stale for either lack of use or just plain no use at all. And furthermore, God did not want our powers of imagination and creativity to function in a robotic way. Have you ever seen a kid and their interaction with the world? Don't they notice the strangest things in the room first that nobody else sees? It is this ability to place themselves into that fantasy environment that sustains them through any challenging time in life.

We should strive to make use of all of the senses that God has blessed us with in this life. Too many people choose to limit God's blessings and plans to what they can see on the horizon. I chose to look beyond what I can see, hear, or feel because those are only a temporary sensations. I want to look at every setback, every disappointment, and every trial as a setup for a date with destiny!!

Does this mean that every cloud chased will lead to fair skies? No. Will my life all of sudden be free from trials and error? Not exactly. But what is clear is my vision. A vision is something that we all need to reexamine every year to see areas where we have changed, grown, or regressed since last formulating that statement. This vision is something that nobody can steal or hinder you from accomplishing if you believe in what God will do through you today. Phil 1:6 NKJV states that "Being confident of this very thing, that He who has begun a good work in you will complete it until the day of Jesus Christ" You and I, my friends, are still under construction!! This is great news because Jesus is refining and digging new channels through the old pathways of our minds and hearts for His glory. He is personally laying out every branch to our heart and those branches are eventually going to blossom into something beyond your wildest dreams.

John 21 records the story of the disciples going out to catch fish. It is nightfall in the camp and the disciples had been fishing the whole night without a single fish to show in their quivers. How is it these "skilled fisherman" ended up with dry empty nests? They had watched countless video from the experts on their stone tablets, they read the latest farmer's almanac dreaming of nets bursting with fish, and lastly the brought their friends along for the ride to share in the joy of fishing. There is nothing like having a friend there to take a mental photograph of all that you have accomplished. Nightfall began to descend upon the horizon. It would appear that switching baits or tactics would make the most sense after so many hours of empty nets. After all, when you know a lake or area so well, sometimes things become a bit too familiar. Have you ever told someone it will never work because you were looking at the same plans for too long? Have you ever witnessed a doctor tell parents that their baby needs a miracle to survive in their estimation? Have someone ever told you that cannot be something because it is just not in you or because of a test you failed? But in the midst of all this "darkness" surrounding them out there, Jesus is walking along the shore calmly and patiently waiting for the disciples to acknowledge him. I think Jesus has a great sense of humor. If you and I had been fishing all night and did not catch anything but woke up to the smell of fish, would you not be mad? I would have run over to Jesus, so you are just going to have a fish fillet with bread and hummus in front of me today huh? You could not wait until my friends were gone home for the day?

But alas, no fish, just an empty net with a little crab's running back into the vast salty haven of blue they call home sweet home. How many times have we followed the same routine, protocol, or plans only to wind up with empty nets in our lives? How many times have we failed to toss out the empty nets still clinging to the fibers of our hearts, minds, and souls? Jesus wants us to stop chasing and rehashing empty nets and cast out of our comfort zones into area where the fishes of joy, success, peace, and emotional healing are ripe for harvesting. Sometimes the only way to see light through the darkness is to keep your eyes focused on the last place you saw the light. In other words, your success depends on being willing to follow and obey Jesus, the Light, no matter what path He takes you on in this life. It could involve making some adjustments to the bait you are using to spread the love of Christ or promote your gifts and talents to the world. It could also involve leaving behind old friends whose only possibilities or forecast for you include the words "failure" and "not acceptable".

Secondly, it is important to open your heart to the possibility that the open and uncharted waters in your life contain. It is not the bad fear of things that might make you afraid but instead it is the fear of the excitement of what lies ahead for you. Sometimes this open approach lends itself to taking advice from people who you normally who not have listened to in the past. It might come in the form of a relative or best friend that is always joking about you coming with them to sing in the choir, join a salsa club, play in the orchestra, or practice for running a marathon. Take and cherish every encounter with your friends and family and the advice that they give to you on a daily basis.

Furthermore, one of the greatest blessings is knowing that you have a friend to share in the highs and lows of this new experience. It helps to show you that it is okay to stumble a bit and laugh at yourself while you are still learning the ropes. It helps everyone to see that you are human and they are human as well. It is good to know that even though one stream of your life did not yield much fruit, there are still so many more streams yet still unexplored and untapped by you.

If you want to attract the right people who can help you do any task, then you have to place yourself in an environment that is ripe for making your dreams a reality. I remember my college banquet days with both joy and apprehension. It was a cool late February. Our banquet only came around once per year and so that made it extra special to everyone. I had a hard time asking for a date this year because I wanted to go out with a particular young lady who happened to be one of the most popular and beautiful ladies in our junior class. I was sure that she has heard all of the smooth lines and guys attempting to ask her out all of the time. In fact, she probably has a catalog of responses in her mind to thwart such advances to avoid those guys she deems as "rejects". During lunchtime at the café, I would casually joke about asking her out to the banquet. 'Hey guys, I am to ask her out to the banquet, just watch me'. "Yea, you mean in your mind you had asked her out", barked Steve one of my friends at the table. A nervous laughter splashed across my face for a brief second followed by a stern smirk. I had about four weeks before the banquet and so time was not an issue to implement my plan. Doubts began to fill my mind like smoke as I thought to myself 'What do I have to offer this lady that she A. Cannot find in another young man or B. have a reason to somehow skip those guys and choose me for a banquet date. I decided I that I needed to clear my head and so I went running around the campus with my IPod firmly attached to my arm blazing the latest contemporary gospel and jazz. There is something about great music that is both relaxing and inspiring.

After a 5k, I returned tired. My roommate began inquiring why I had not been as proactive when asking this young lady out. I told him that I cannot see her accepting my invitation to go to the banquet especially after receiving all of the negative vibes from my close friends earlier that day in the café. He proceeded to tell me to just do it!! "Just do it", he shouted from the top of his lungs. I began to laugh because all of this time I was devising this ultimate plan to get her to accept my invitation without reservations. Let's face nobody likes to be considered a "last option" or conversely a "pity date" consolation. You know what a pity date is:

some young lady who felt sorry for you like you were a cute puppy dog that she could not refuse. My roommate was the go getter type and he does not hold anything back and I appreciated that the most about him.

I asked her the next day after class and she said yes!! I was grateful for the good time we had at that banquet. But more importantly, I was more grateful for the opportunity to reach out of my comfort zone and experience a new friend even till this day we still talk and share experiences with one another. I wish I can say that it ended in marriage but that would be a lie!! I am sure she married someone just like me, I hope ☺

So how can you prepare to open your hearts to the possibilities practically today in your life?

1. Be fearless and step out your comfort zone by becoming active in an event or hobby you have never done before in your life. Things like skydiving, art shows, music festivals, book clubs, car clubs, sports etc… You will feel less self-conscious because everyone is in the same boat as you- beginners and loving every minute of it!! And you cannot say you do not like something, you have not tried yet. 2 Timothy 1:7 NKJV says "For God has not given us the spirit of fear, but of power, and of love, and of a sound mind". Use the equipment God has already blessed you with today!!

2. Be positive about every situation you find yourself in no matter how steep the mountain of negativity might look. There is a short poem that goes like this:

Love has 4 letter, but so does hate. Friends has 7 letters but so does Enemies; Truth has 5 letters but so does Lying, Hurt has 4 letters, but so does Heal-

(Unknown) It's all in our perspective in how we view things and our reaction to those things that makes all of the difference in this world. Proverbs 17:22 NKJV tells us "A merry heart does good like medicine, but a broken spirit dries the bones".

3. Surround yourself with new friends and old friends and family who are "sharpeners". Sharpeners are those people who refine you and make you better by telling you the truth about yourself and helping you to maximize your gifts and talents toward God's optimal for your life. Proverbs 27:17 NKJV states "As iron sharpens iron, so a man sharpens the countenance of a friend".

4. Keep track of your progress like baby steps and development. A visual record serves as both a motivator and provides a sense of accomplishment showing you how far you have come in the past! 1 Timothy 4:15 NKJV "Mediate on these things; give yourself entirely to them so that your progress may be evident to all".

5. Create a prayer group at your church or after school friends to pray for everyone to meet new people and pray for their success in any new venture. This group can meet at your house, a friend's house, or sometime after church service and plan to do something special like making a card, sending a gift card, or doing something for a different person in the group every other week depending on what their issue is that month.

6. Visit a homeless shelter, nursing home, or mall outlet and offer your gift/talent to others free of charge. You never know who might be there as well as the great advice and blessings you will get by being there. Matthew 25:40 NKJV states "

And the King will answer and say to them, Assuredly I say to you, inasmuch as you did it to one of the least of my brethren, you did it to me".

7. Finally, and most importantly, keep Jesus at the center of your vision and plans by letting Him direct you to waters fill of fish and opportunity in your life. Do this by praying three times or more a day and inviting Him into your heart daily. Matt 6:35 NKJV "But seek first the kingdom of God and His righteousness, and all these things shall be added unto you

JoyRX Action Questions

1. When was the last time that you worked on your dreams unashamedly?

2. How many people have you encouraged their dreams, goals, and plans?

3. What do you think is possible with God's help in your life today?

4. What projects have you placed on hold due to a "rainy day"?

Chapter 5 Now Hiring Joy Ambassadors: No Previous Experience Needed!!

Have you ever hated your job before and wished that you were doing something else? Do you sometimes feel undervalued, unappreciated, and definitely underpaid at your current job? Its ok you can admit it, nobody checking you!! Well there is much to be said about being in a place where you are not happy and not feeling like you are using the talents God has given you.

My first job was a bagger at a grocery store. I envied my other friends who had plush office jobs as secretaries and those who go to work strictly indoors. My work was monotonous, tiresome, and repetitive. I was not allowed to accept tips of any kind. I am not the type of person to enjoy robotic work without much interaction with people normally. Imagine having to smile while lifting items such as heavy watermelons, boxes, and crates of food out to a customer's car only to have them yell at you for dropping the bananas on the pavement of which the store would replace for free anyway. The customers that really annoyed me where the ones who requested special items that they knew our store did not carry or the ones who wanted their groceries bagged with plastic inside of paper. My boss seemed more like Pharaoh and his taskmaster ways irked me as he stood over me waiting for me to break something so he could fire me on the spot. But I was one of the most proficient and fastest baggers in that store, not that it made me any more special. My college acceptance letters were not exactly rolling down like the Niagara, and for all intents and purposes, I felt stuck!! I needed to eat because my parents come from the school of 'You don't work, you don't eat'. I was mildly depressed at any other future prospects looming on the horizon. The only consolation prize here was that work was within walking distance from my house.

But things began to change about six months into my gig, I now realized that I was placing too much emphasis on my own happiness and that I was too selfish at work with my workmates and with those outside of work. I thought about all of the customers I interacted with on a daily basis, how are they feeling when they enter this store? Are they stressed out after work, having to juggle kids in their shopping basket, and just having a bad day? It was my privilege and opportunity to provide them with a brighter experience since I would technically be the last face they see as the exited the store. When food and people interact in a store, positive things normally follow.

I began to smile more and talk to customers while they were standing in the line. I would help them make the best selection on food items and direct them to the appropriate manger when they needed to vent about something in the store. The grocery store is one of the best places to meet new people and learn from them because everybody has to eat. My boss began to take notice and he had me do the daily announcements over the intercom highlighting our famous French baked bread. Some customers would shop at one store for everything else and then drive twenty minutes or more to get their hands on our always fresh, hot, and soft French bread. I miss that bread!

I did not think that smiling and making my customer's lives a bit easier for a moment was a talent for God but God uses the little things to do mighty works in our lives!! I began to witness to the power of God when taking out my customers groceries and some would even give me Bible tracts or just say an encouraging word to help me through the day. I was not only just "doing my job" but now my gifts and talents were being woven into my job to form a beautiful symphony of expression and passion for others in my community.

Sometimes we have to invest the talents, gifts, and time that God has given us no matter what situation we find ourselves in. We may not see the results or dividends immediately, but somebody is always paying attention and you will a harvest in due season.

There was another person who did not have a great situation to begin with but they made "lemons out of lemonade". In Acts 15, there is the story of the Jerusalem Council- a meeting of early Christians and Jews trying to decide should new believers be circumcised? There was a lot of tension and strife between the two groups. But there was two people who changed the outcome from negative to a positive report and their names were Judas and Silas. It was their sole job to be the encouragers of the Christian brethren of Antioch.

How would you like that for a job? It was the best thing because words are powerful, specially the spoken word. They did not take their task lightly and probably stayed a long time with those believers answering questions and giving sound advice to the believers. It is a good thing to be able to hear and witness someone giving a good report amidst all the chaos and distractions that we all face in the world today.

Lessons Learned from Judas and Silas

The first lesson learned is that these men did not hesitate to go on the mission that they were assigned. They were prophets themselves and could have written a letter but they chose to deliver the message and speak encouraging words to the brethren at Antioch, It is important to invest and develop the gifts and talents that God has given us already for His glory. Do not try to start from scratch so to speak and invest time and energy in a role that you were not destined by God to play. Sometimes some people feel that the gift or talent they have is not as important or higher ranked in their mind as the next person but this is not true at all.

Secondly, by investing in helping others, it opens the gateway for our own souls to be revived and refreshed by God. It does not take much to impact the lives of those less fortunate than you. I recall a time when I went to visit a soup kitchen on a Sunday morning. It was not the serving of food that warmed my heart for truly any robot can do that!! But it was the conversation with the people there seasoned with life stories and experiences. At the end of the day, everyone just want a chance to be heard and contribute to the fabric of life's story through service to their fellow human beings. It touched my heart to see the spirit of determination and cooperation amongst some of the people that we served that Sunday morning. If you invest in helping others, you might be surprised as they will fill up your proverbial tank to get you through that Monday morning test that's lurking right around the corner.

Furthermore, you must be willing to risk all in this investment of happiness. Paul and Silas were not interested in giving a half report, doing a halfhearted job, or even making a name for themselves in the ancient world. They were totally committed to the project of furthering the gospel of Jesus Christ by promoting unity and encouragement to their fellow brethren. It is tempting to "fake it till you make it" or only make those happy who have pasted a smile on your face in the past. You and I must be willing to give 100 percent for the sake of making those around us happy in this life.

JoyRX Action Questions to Consider

1. How can I invest in volunteering my time for others in service to my community or church?

2. When was the last time I used my talents or gifts to help my neighbor or classmate?

3. What is the one thing holding you back from sharing with others what God has blessed you with?

4. Where can you serve today with your gift (a school, church, gym, band, job, etc..) toda

Chapter 6 Joy Killers Drop Those Weights

One of my favorite cartoons as a kid was the Pinky and the Brain series that came on as part of the show Animaniacs. The show featured two lab mice who lived in a cage in Acme labs. Pinky was the fun loving, easygoing, and mindless one who just wanted to live in the moment. Brain was a schemer and dreamer whose only thoughts centered on making his plans a reality in the near future. Brain was a smart individual perhaps too smart for his own good. He came across to some as arrogant and others viewed him as focused and determined as his confidence in a successful outcome never wavered no matter how hard the winds of pessimism blew.

Pinky would gallantly and sometimes naively ask

"Gee, Brain, what do you want to do tonight?"

To which Brain would respond "The same thing we do every night, Pinky- try to take over the world!"

Everyone else watching Brain's plans unfold episode after episode knew that the plans would fail but Brain would push forward believing one day to set free from Acme Labs. Pinky would be ever faithful in providing support although at times he would sabotage Brain's plans of action. This "dynamic duo" each had different visions of life but they always supported one another despite the sarcasm and banter between them at times. Do you sometimes find yourself distracted from your dreams and plans due to the air of negativity you breathe in from others?

Granted Brain's dreams were not the easiest to fulfill and taking over the world was never accomplished but it is his spirit of determination in the face of obvious obstacles that motivated viewers and kids to watch all of the episodes. If a person is not helping you toward your goals, then they are a hindrance like dead weights filled with water instead of strong concrete. You have to be willing to cut out those people who are talking or working against you on your road to recovery and success. Some can be great motivators but others are just constantly negative and it will affect your performance in everything if they continue to hound all of your projects and plans in life.

I remember when I was my freshman year in a public high school. The school that I attended did not have the latest books, they did not offer an advanced computer lab or state of the art media center. In fact our school district was on the national fail list in terms of the state standardized tests that was given every year to students. Most teachers would try to motivate their students to study and do well but that fell against deaf ears. Most parents were looking for ways to transfer their kids away from our school even if that meant moving to a new school zone. But I had dreams of becoming lawyer, specifically an environmental lawyer that would defend against illegal dumping of chemicals in both urban and rural areas. I would dream of sitting and defending cases on the Supreme Court of the United States. I went to every event dealing with social science that I could think of just to practice public speaking skills.

But one day in my world history professor, of whom I admired, began to challenge my dreams and plans. Let's flashback to the first day of class to get the backdrop. I was a good student, not great, because I was thought of to be the class jokster most of the time. It was not that I did not like the class or the professor. It was just that the class was boring. Not boring in the classical sense, I mean boring like sleeping on your desk while the monotous teacher's voice snakes past your ears slowing than honey dripping out a honeycomb. This was only exscabted by the class being two hours long- I mean how much world history can one absorb without a total brain meltdown?

One day he saw me chatting to my friend sitting across from me during his lecture and his eyes pierced my chest like a radar gone astray. "Anthony, why don't you tell us the answer to what period of dinosaur's era we are now in?" I peered nervously around the room hoping that someone else would help a brother out. Silence filled the cavity of this space and I knew that the answer I gave did not matter but detention was going to be the standard dose of the day for me. "Uhm, I have seen Barney and he is a big dinosaur on TV, that's the only one that I know of at this time!!" The room erupted in laughter like a kid whose just been tickled to death by his loving mother. I thought it was funny too but the teacher stood, arms folded, steam rising from his shiny bold forehead, and at that moment I knew hot air was about to burst forth from his lips of wisdom and grandeur. "That's incorrect, and you know what maybe you should read more of my textbook, who knows, you might actually become smarter!!" And so that was the beginning of a challenging relationship with my teacher. I apologized to him the next day but I realized that it was not that, he honestly did not believe that I was capable of learning world history or passing his class for that matter. I began to read to book and raise my hands to answer questions in class and the teacher would make fun of my right answers or ignore my hand for another student. I grew frustrated because history was one of the few subjects on my schedule that I enjoyed going to class every day.

Things went from worse to worst when I found out that he referred me to take counseling tests by the counselor. This was before the days of ADHD. I walked into the counselor's room and began the career test of what I thought would go smoothly. The test came back as said that I was not cut out for college level work and the list of suggested careers proved dismal as well.

I was hurt, upset, and confused because I wanted a chance to prove that I was just as smart as everyone else in my class. My parents and I did not believe the results of any test. Most of the other teachers wanted to put me into special education classes, not because I was slow, but because they felt that I would just cause too much distraction and not learn the material they were presenting. I was determined to not let that counselor or my teacher had the last word.

After all, "with God all things are possible" and this certainly proved the case here as well. My parents fought to keep me in regular classes and I did my part as well by studying for success in all of my subjects and not just the ones that I liked. I wish I could say I made straight A's that year but I would be lying!!

I passed to the next grade and by next school year my parents transferred me to a private junior academy. It was there that I began to excel due to the excellent Christian teachers and their personalized attention to learning and success. I soon became a top student and made it to college to study and graduate on time in four years as well. If I had chosen to internalize those experiences in my freshman year, I would be totally discouraged from even trying to learn academically on any level. It is always great to know that what God has blessed you with can never be taken away from you by the schemes and plans of others.

But the journey involves making tough choices and cutting out those negative feelings and pasting in positive choices daily. It involves making decisions to press forward in the beginning when everybody else is saying they cannot see any blessing on your horizon. It means continuing to study biochemistry Saturday night while everyone else is out ice skating. It means paying that tithe when you know your car payment is due and everyone is saying pay it or else! It means avoiding those who constantly bring you down through the words and actions. Everyone has bad days and that's permissible as a human, however some people constantly carry around negativity like a dripping rain cloud that never fades away.

Job experienced the worst possible scenario that would have caused some people to recant their faith in God. We know the story: Job gets tempted by the Devil to curse God and in doing so loses his health, his children, his sheep and oxen, and most of his livelihood. If anything you would expect support from your better half, your best friend, aka the wife, but alas not even she tells him to "curse God and die".

But more importantly Job's friends probe the mysteries of why Job is being attacked so severely by the Devil. To their credit, they first comfort him for seven days not speaking by just empathizing with Job. You know sometimes just being there for someone without making suggestions, improvements, or refinement is the antidote needed for a friend. But later on in the story, Job's friends began to question and probe what Job might have done to cause such misfortune to come about in his life. They began to insinuate that it was something Job had done and begged him to confess it before God. When times get rough, you need to know that "there is a Friend that sticketh closer than a brother" The last thing you want to hear with boils begging to be itched on your body is that you caused all of this chaos yourself. Sometimes friends can amplify the level of negativity that you are already facing. It is then vital that you do not believe their talk or even your own talk against yourself. You, like Job, have to know when to part ways with those who only mean evil for you and not good. You need a made up mind that you will follow God's plans for your life even if you do not have a fan's appreciation box waiting for you on the other side.

I council you that God will send you new friends who will love you just the way you are and will not change your visions and dreams. So let's begin to cut out negative thoughts and actions from others in our lives today!

Practical Ways to Overcome Negative People and Situations

1. Make or draw a diagram that lists all of the positive traits, attributes, and talents that God has given to you. If you can't think of many, then have your closest friend's list one thing that they admire about you. Take this and hang it on your wall or refrigerator for everyone to see.

2. Trust your God given instincts, don't quit on anything, and follow through with all your plans and dreams. There is a time and season for everything and your season for growth and change might be just around the corner.

3. Pray for those negative people and situations. Visit those friends or call them if they are far away and just ask if there is anything they would like to pray about and have them pray for you as well.

4. Welcome constructive criticism and affirm the people providing this kind of feedback to you always by acknowledging and implementing their advice.

5. Let go quickly of those situations and people that might lead you to do something you will regret for a long time by thinking of another positive experience you have had in the past that day.

6. Kill the person or their influencing friends with kindness going out of your way to make them comfortable. Do the opposite of what they expect and watch how things simmer down in the long run.

7. Believe in yourself always by focusing on your strengths and bringing out the best in others at all times. The negativity shown could just be a wish by the other person to know how to use their talents and gifts to the fullest like you are currently doing in your capacity.

JoyRX Questions to Consider

1. How often are you thinking about negative situations before you even try to change your situation?

2. When was the last time you stepped out in faith and committed to a project?

3. How many of your friends and family do you need to stop hanging around or listening to for a while?

4. What would you do now if you have no critics or detractors from your plan?

Chapter 7 Just Breathing My Way Through

Zoom, Zoom, Zoom!!, this was the sounds of a symphony composed of cars, vans, trucks, and RV's that raced past on a freeway suspended above my neighborhood. It is the scene of approximately 300,000 cars per day traveling along the 405 every day. It is the constant noise of motion that invades the cavities of our senses until we are swept up in its undercurrents. People everywhere moving along the sideways, streets, and alleyways of America entangled in a constant stream of motion and stress increasing environments.

In addition to this, when a person finally reaches their destination, they are fed a steady diet of constant projects, proposals, papers, deadlines, and a myriad of other tasks designed to sap their souls vitality from them at any moment's notice. The individual then resorts to eating a bag lunch in a cubicle full of papers and gulping the cola from the 7-11 morning rush hour. Returning home after

Was life designed to move at the speed of sound? Is there a better way to increase productivity and still live life somewhat happy? I am guilty of spreading myself too thin too many times myself whether its joining too many clubs at school or trying to please everybody in one setting or another.

Luke 5:16 NKJV tells us that Jesus often withdrew to lonely and distant places in order to be with the Father. This is the time He used to recharge and reflect on His mission. In this world, it seems weird to stand still for any one period of time. We are raised to do more, be more, say more, give more, move more, and love more. But have you ever thought about the notion of doing less to do more in the future. Jesus constantly maintained that connection with the Father so that when He did miracles and wonders they were numerous and life changing as well. In fact the Bible says that so many were done that all of it could not be recorded. "And there were also many other things Jesus did, which if were written one by one, I suppose that even the world itself could not contain the books that would be written. Amen." John 21:26 NKJV

I love to weightlift and exercise for fun and also for relaxation after a long day of work and studying. While lifting heavy weights on the bench press, it is important that you breathe in and out properly in order to avoid injury or just plain uncomfortableness. It is also imperative that you take you take your time moving slowly through the repetitions while maintaining proper form at all times.

I remember my sophomore year in college, we all were required to take a PE class elective in order to graduate on time. I took weightlifting thinking it would be an easy elective as well as get my body ready for the summer beach season. I was so excited that my class contained four women, two of which I was very interested in at the time. I wanted to impress them and the perfect opportunity was coming at the bench press test for our class by our instructor. I went to the gym on my off class days and rushed through the different weights like a bottle of soda pop opened too fast. I wore my muscle shirts to the café at dinner time. I brought the whey protein shakes and drank them once a day in the morning. I felt good hearing the murmurs of the girls as they saw me in the café and elsewhere.

The day had finally come and I wore my best workout attire to the gym that day. At least if I don't lift that much I will look good for the yearbook photo staff that could be there. My classmate's places 180 on the bar and my scrawny frame curled under the bar like a caterpillar unwilling to unwind too fast. I breathed in and out twice and then lifted the bar with help from the spotter. I pressed it down without breathing and felt a thud on my chest. I tried to pull the bar up but the only thing moving was the hairs on my chest!! I had not probably breathed in and out and went too fast trying to press out as many repetitions as I could to impress the girls. I was embarrassed and still to this day have the bar marks on my chest!! Well maybe not on my chest physically but mentally!

Exercise and rest can be an aphrodisiac to combat all of the stress and worry that we all face on a daily basis. It is important that we all take time to enjoy life, the process of growing, learning, and trying new things again. It sometimes feel like we do not have a moment to catch our breath but this is precisely what is needed in order to get more done in life.

Here are some suggestions for enjoying life and taking things more slowly in a fast paced world:

1. Take a nature walk and camp out with your significant other or loved one at a special park of your choice.

2. Enroll in an exercise class whether it be kickboxing, Pilates, or some other aerobics class.

3. Play with your kids, grandkids, or other kids in the neighborhood the favorite sport of their choice.

4. Learn to laugh at yourself and others you observe in the park, mall, school, or work doing not so serious things.

5. Construct one space in your house or around your yard where you can meet God each day to talk about your day and exhale all of your stress away.

JoyRX Questions to Consider

1. What things in my life are distractions or diversions from helping me to reach me goals and dreams?

2. When was the last time you took a weekend trip with family and friends to the beach or somewhere relaxing?

3. Do you feel more relaxed after exercising, running, biking, swimming, kickboxing, etc.?

4. Where is your special place of solitude where you can relax and get the most done in an hour or day?

5. Do you find yourself in a hurry to accomplish little or is better to slow down to get more done?

Chapter 8 Where Do I Go From Here?

Philippians 3:12-14 NKJV ^{Not} that I have already attained, or am already perfected; but I press on, that I may lay hold of that for which Christ Jesus has also laid hold of me. Brethren, I do not count myself to have apprehended; but one thing *I do,* forgetting those things which are behind and reaching forward to those things which are ahead, I press toward the goal for the prize of the upward call of God in Christ Jesus.

Life in a snapshot is about a constant state of motion and progress toward a point in time, a goal, a dream, a mission, a calling, or a destiny. It has always amazed me to watch things like traffic for instance, you see cars leaving and entering the expressway like ants in constant motion, and they do not slow down for anything even if an accident or dead animal is in the middle of the freeway. Still others of us choose to bike, fly, or take a ship across the seven seas on this planet. In all these cases, the thought never initially crosses our minds that our so called forward progress would be stopped or halted. We assume that our cars no matter how old or maintenance neglected will help us to reach our final destination. We assume that our method of transportation is just as sure as the ground we are walking on. Admittedly, any interruption in our daily routine in life is uncomfortable, inconvenient, annoying, and painful. If you don't believe me try waiting an extra second before hitting the gas on a green light, or seeing people's reactions after an overnight flight delay, or even just watching siblings play with one toy too long at the expense of the other.

It takes a mountain of patience to bear with the ups and downs of life's trajectory. I love to run half marathons and just running in general. During these races, two things usually happen to frustrate my forward progress: First, I start out too fast above my normal pace trying to keep up with others that I end up running out of steam by the fifth mile. Second, I get so focused and in the zone that I get lost on the track and have to wait for the other runners to lead the way home. I sometimes envy those perfect runners who finish way ahead of the pack. Why can't they just win by a runner's length to make it interesting for the fans? Why come in so far ahead of the pack? So I asked one elite runner, 'Why do you keep running so hard even when you are a mile ahead of everyone else, isn't your victory already sure? He responded by saying 'I always aim to beat my own personal record and in fact still racing against myself. I am running against myself always.' Wow, that sounds like a runner with purpose, dedication, and commitment even though it seems some success is already in his hands. There is a desire in all of our hearts that draws us toward Christ, the one who can give us all everlasting joy. He has been running after us since the beginning of time and now it is time for us to catch up to His long arms of mercy to finish this race!!

So how can we finish this race toward healing and recovery in our lives today? Here are 7 practical suggestions to get us off the starting blocks today!

1. Run your race, not someone else's and acknowledge that you are under construction. Don't be a copycat, shine in your own God given talents. "He who has begun a good work in you will complete it until the end" Phil 1:6

2. Forget the Past- Sometimes we forget that Christ has forgiven us completely and wants us to be with Him always!! Do not look back like Lot's wife while running toward Christ at things you wish you had or things that have easily beset you in the past. Because looking causes us to stumble, pause, or stop completely. Jesus said that you are "a new creature in Him, old things are passed away Corinthians 5:17. Christ states "Behold, I make all things new" Revelation 21:1

3. Focus- You must keep your focus on the prize which is heaven!! This road of life is not meant to be a smooth journey because it's temporary. Do not feel slighted by the bumps of defeat, opposition, and lonely nights and days. In a race sometimes we all have the tendency to look at those around us who may be running faster or slower than us. You cannot focus on things on the sidelines such as possessions, power, and prestige. You cannot focus on the haters on the sidelines. You must have tunnel vision for Christ, Christ must be your Magnificent Obsession. But God requires that we focus on Him as He did

45

when He was on earth. Phil 3:10 Paul states his ultimate focus "that I may know Him and the Power of His Resurrection".

4. Finish Strong- This is the most important part of the journey. It is not enough just to barely finish something whether it is a marathon or in the race of life. Jesus gives us the ability to excel in any race by His Spirit. The Holy Spirit is your Second Wind. The Holy Spirit is your Gatorade. He states "not by might, nor by power, but by my Spirit says the Lord Almighty. Jesus will run in front of you to clear the obstacles of bills, exams, wayward kids, depression, loneliness, troubled spouses, evil bosses, bad health, broken down cars, broken down houses, etc…Jesus will run behind to defend you from the potholes and other runners vying to trip you up before the finish line. But most importantly, Jesus will CARRY OUT across and beyond the finish line in your race of life.

5. Become a support system and knowledge bank for others as a joy ambassador on the trail. Encourage your fellow runners through situations and terrain that you have already traversed before and let them know you are praying for their success and happiness too!

6. Refuel daily with the water of the Word of God and the energy bars of the Holy Spirit to give you that second wind daily. Make this your number one station that you visit early morning and late at night and at all points in the middle also.

7. Cloth yourself with peace and love every day. The fires of love and peace will become as contagious as a crowd performing the wave in support of all the runners.

8. Be consistently looking for ways to use the gifts and talents that God has given you even in the smallest of venues or arenas. You will not only be blessing yourself but others as well in the process.

9. Recruit a partner, not just any partner, but one who will look out for your best interests and be a coach when you call at 2am in the morning and nobody is watching you.

10. Enjoy the process, slow down, breathe, and thank God for the progress He has already made in your life. Keep a voice recorder handy on your phone and listen to it on the way to work, school, or the mall of all of the ways God has blessed you this week, month, or year.

JoyRX Questions to Consider

1. What is the one area of your life that needs to be revised, improved, or given an extreme makeover in terms of your outlook on life?
2. When would you like to commit to living in the everlasting joy that Christ has planned for you?
3. How has rejoicing helped you or a friend through times of grief, pain, or difficulty in the past?
4. How giving or providing joy and happiness to others does affected your own journey thus far in life?
5. What or who is keeping you from experiencing God's best for you right now?